The Powys Brothers

by R. C. CHURCHILL

Published for The British Council
and The National Book League
by Longmans, Green & Co.

Two shillings and sixpence net

The 150th issue in the *Writers and Their Work* series, the first number of which appeared in June 1950, honours a remarkable contemporary family.

The three brothers Powys considered by Mr. Churchill are John Cowper Powys, who has just attained the age of ninety, an occasion which brought him world-wide congratulation; Theodore Powys, novelist and story-teller, who died nearly ten years ago; and Llewelyn Powys, a versatile writer who was the shortest lived of the three, though perhaps the widest in his interests. The bibliography contributed by Mr. Maurice Hussey includes books by brothers and sisters of the celebrated trio.

Mr. Churchill concurs with most critics that Theodore Powys was the most original of the brethren, but one of the merits of his essay is that he presents a balanced view of their diverse accomplishments.

Bibliographical Series
of Supplements to 'British Book News'
on Writers and Their Work

★

GENERAL EDITOR
Bonamy Dobrée

JOHN COWPER
POWYS

LLEWELLYN
POWYS

T. F. POWYS

THE POWYS BROTHERS

by

R. C. CHURCHILL

I well remember once hearing in a town in Iowa about a very philosophical, very gentlemanly, and very learned recluse, whose favourite writer was 'Powys'. I wonder if Theodore and Llewelyn have the same odd sensation when they hear or see the word 'Powys', and learn that it does not refer to themselves?

JOHN COWPER POWYS: *Autobiography*.

PUBLISHED FOR
THE BRITISH COUNCIL
and the NATIONAL BOOK LEAGUE
by LONGMANS, GREEN & CO.

LONGMANS, GREEN & CO. LTD.,
48 Grosvenor Street, London, W.1.
Railway Crescent, Croydon, Victoria, Australia
Auckland, Kingston (Jamaica), Lahore, Nairobi

LONGMANS SOUTHERN AFRICA (PTY) LTD.
Thibault House, Thibault Square, Cape Town,
Johannesburg, Salisbury

LONGMANS OF NIGERIA LTD.
W.R. Industrial Estate, Ikeja

LONGMANS OF GHANA LTD.
Industrial Estate, Ring Road, South Accra

LONGMANS GREEN (FAR EAST) LTD.
443 Lockhart Road, Hong Kong

LONGMANS OF MALAYA LTD.
44 Jalan Ampang, Kuala Lumpur

ORIENT LONGMANS LTD.
Calcutta, Bombay, Madras
Delhi, Hyderabad, Dacca

LONGMANS CANADA LTD.
137 Bond Street, Toronto 2

Printed in Great Britain by
F. Mildner & Sons, London, E.C.1

CONTENTS

¶ JOHN COWPER POWYS was born at Shirley Vicarage, Shirley, near Ashbourne, Derbyshire, in 1872 and now lives in Merionethshire, North Wales; THEODORE FRANCIS POWYS was born at Shirley Vicarage in 1875 and died at Mappowder, near Sturminster Newton, Dorsetshire, in 1953; LLEWELYN POWYS was born at Rothesay House, Dorchester, Dorsetshire, in 1884 and died at Clavadel Sanatorium, Davos-Platz, Switzerland, in 1939.

THE POWYS BROTHERS

I

THE BRONTËS AND THE POWYSES

LITERATURE, unlike music, does not often run in families. There are many Bachs, but only one Dante; a whole family of Strauss, but a single Shakespeare, a solitary Voltaire. Among the English exceptions to this general rule, the Brontë sisters and the Powys brothers are the most remarkable; and it is natural to enquire whether the two families have anything in common besides this.

The most obvious common factor leads to the chief difference. Charlotte, Emily and Anne Brontë were the daughters of the Rev. Patrick Brontë, a Church of England clergyman of Evangelical outlook who was the son of an Irish peasant farmer called Branty or Brunty; their mother came from a Cornish Methodist family, so they had Celtic ancestry on both sides. John Cowper, Theodore Francis and Llewelyn Powys were of similar clerical origin, being the sons of the Rev. Charles Francis Powys (1843-1923), a Church of England clergyman of Evangelical views who was descended from a branch of the ancient Welsh family of Powys, intermarried in recent centuries with English and Swiss stock; their mother, Mary Cowper Johnson (1849-1914), was of part English, part Irish-German descent, on her father's side related to that famous Norfolk family which had given to literature the Jacobean poet John Donne, Dean of St. Paul's, and William Cowper, the greatest Evangelical poet of the eighteenth century. The Victorian novelist sisters and the twentieth-century novelist brothers have in common, therefore, a clerical, mainly Evangelical background and a large measure of Celtic blood.

Of the value of the Celtic inheritance, crossed as it was by English environment and upbringing—in Yorkshire in the case of the Brontës, principally in Somerset and Dorset

7

in the case of the Powyses—there is ample evidence to be found in their writings. The clerical and Evangelical inheritance, however, worked in a contrary direction in the Powys brothers to that which it took in the Brontës. John Cowper Powys became a mystic philosopher, who rejects conventional Christianity but nevertheless feels, like Bloody Johnny in his *Glastonbury Romance*, that the material universe is not all; the philosophy which informs the novels and stories of T. F. Powys may be briefly described as pantheism with an heretical Christian accent; while Llewelyn Powys, believing that 'Christianity teaches us to despise life', became a militant Atheist whose book *The Pathetic Fallacy* accuses the Church of distorting the simple teachings of Jesus and who preached in *Damnable Opinions*, 'the hand-book of my beliefs', a gospel of happiness on earth that rejects the Christian doctrine of immortality. Some aspects of *Wuthering Heights* and *Jane Eyre* may not have been altogether to the taste of the Rev. Patrick Brontë, but his daughters lived and died in the Christian faith in which they had been brought up. The Powys brothers, by contrast, reveal an almost complete break with their clerical inheritance. T. F. Powys, it is true, read the lessons in East Chaldon church for nearly forty years, but his acknowledged masterpieces in fiction—*Mr. Weston's Good Wine*, the *Fables* and *Unclay*—reveal an attitude towards Christianity which no clergyman, however broad or modern in outlook, could fully condone.

But this production of heretics from a clerical root had nothing in common with the classic Victorian case of Samuel Butler. (And the root had its revenge, the clerical collar came full circle, when John Cowper's son became a clergyman, like his grandfather, great-grandfather and great-great-grandfather.) There was little repression, comparable to that recorded in Butler's *Way of All Flesh*, about the childhood of the Powys brothers; on the contrary, the happiness of the Powys family life, and the deep affection of all its members for each other, is evident from John

Cowper's *Autobiography* and Llewelyn's *Skin for Skin*, confirmed by their brother Littleton Powys, when he writes that 'though in tastes and interests no two members of the family were alike, in affection for each other they were bound together by bonds which nothing in this world could ever loosen.'* We are reminded, not of the Butler background to *The Way of All Flesh*, but again of the Brontë sisters, not simply because of the similar close affection of the family life but because of the common urge in later years to look back upon their youth. The clannishness of the Powys brothers, which they themselves were the first to recognize, is similar at some points to the closed family circle of the Brontës.

But Charlotte and Anne Brontë are very different writers from Emily, and a gulf of somewhat the same kind separates the *Glastonbury Romance* from the *Fables, Love and Death* from *Mr. Weston's Good Wine*. It is the gulf, in simple terms, separating the romantic and subjective from the more classical, more impersonal. Both John Cowper and Llewelyn Powys are intensely autobiographical writers, whose virtues and faults spring alike from their obsession with their own feelings. They were, moreover, very close to each other in life, even by the remarkably close standards of the Powys family in general; whereas Theodore, by the same remarkably close standards, 'was the most original of the Powys family'—as an American friend once shrewdly put it—'and his originality was such that it inevitably isolated him even from his closest friends and relations.' I shall accordingly consider, together, the writings of the two brothers who were closest in life and in their work, before turning to T. F. Powys, who seems to me the greatest figure, though not all of his writing is on the high level of his comparatively few masterpieces.

* The Rev. C. F. Powys had eleven children in all, including the scholar and sportsman Littleton Charles Powys, the artist Gertrude Mary Powys, who illustrated some of Llewelyn's books, the architect Albert Reginald Powys, and the poet Philippa Powys.

II

JOHN COWPER AND LLEWELYN POWYS

Despite the closeness of the family tie, there is only one work of collaboration in the bibliography of the Powys family, and it seems natural that this should be the *Confessions of Two Brothers* (1916) by John Cowper and Llewelyn. This was Llewelyn's first book, but John Cowper, the eldest of the family, was known as a lecturer in England and America and had published poetry, stories, critical essays and his first novel *Wood and Stone* (1915), in which he mirrored the intimate relationship between himself and Llewelyn in the characters of the brothers Anderson.

The importance of the *Confessions* is twofold: first, that it gave Llewelyn—who had spent seventeen months in a Swiss sanatorium for consumptives from 1909 to 1911 and was now managing his brother William's farm in Kenya— the first sight of his writings in print, an encouragement he needed in order to persevere with his stories and sketches of England and Africa later collected in two of his best books, *Ebony and Ivory* (1923) and *Black Laughter* (1925); secondly, that John Cowper's contributions were a first version of chapters afterwards revised for his *Autobiography* (1934), one of the best and one of the most characteristic of his varied work.

Work varied, that is to say, in outward form. For, in a more inward sense, it is no great exaggeration to describe almost all J. C. Powys's creative work—and some of his critical work too—under the one heading of autobiography. It is not merely in the volume with that title that he reveals himself in all his paradoxical mixture of genuine insight and self-confessed charlatanry. There has always been, by his own admission, a touch of the theatrical about John Cowper Powys: 'There is no use trying to conceal the fact', he writes in the *Autobiography*, 'that Nature from the start had made me an actor.' From youth onward, he has relished his own performance, often observing it, however, with a satirical smile, not altogether taken in by the act but grateful, so to speak, for his privileged seat in the front row. His own complex personality, the various masks he has assumed at different periods of his life, his search for a coherent philosophy which would satisfy his soul, as orthodox Christianity satisfied his beloved father's: these have been the mainspring of his writing for over fifty years.

In the early part of his career, he was mainly known as a lecturer—and by all accounts he was a brilliant one. A protean figure on the platform, his native gifts of wit and eloquence enabled him to share with his audience the fruits of his remarkably wide reading. He tried to get *inside* the author he was discussing:

> In all these lectures . . . [he writes in the *Autobiography*] I worked myself up to such a pitch that I *became* the figure I was analysing . . . I gave myself up to the spirit of my particular man of genius. And it was with almost an erotic emotion, as if I were indulging myself in some kind of perverted love affair, that I entered the nerves of Dickens or Paul Verlaine or Henry James or Dostoievsky or Keats or Blake! . . . My whole idea of *criticism* was different from the academic idea. What I aimed at was a sort of transmigration of my soul, till, like a demon possessing a person, I serpentined myself into the skeleton of my author, and expounded his most eccentric reactions to life from the actual nerve-centres where these reactions originated.

The danger of such an undertaking is, of course, that no critic, however protean his nerve-centres, can be quite certain that in the transmigratory process he has not revealed more of himself than of his author. Dickens, Dostoievsky, Henry James . . . all have a distinct flavour of John Cowper Powys before he has done with them, as G. K. Chesterton imposed his own characteristics upon such varied figures as Cobbett, Browning and St. Thomas Aquinas. We can judge something of the effect of these lectures by reading Powys's published criticisms, such books as *Visions and Revisions* (1915), *Suspended Judgments: Essays on Books and*

Sensations (1916), *The Meaning of Culture* (1930) and *The Pleasures of Literature* (1938). Prolix and repetitive as they are, these books do reveal something of the genius that made the author such a stimulating figure on the platform and such a brilliant conversationalist in private life. The valuable insights are always there, if the reader has to quarry for them among much else.

The prodigal fluency and the genius for introspective digression are seen at their height in the *Autobiography*, but here they can be accepted without much reservation. It was part of Powys's purpose in this remarkable book to disarm criticism by making such a display of his own failings—'my naughty passion', he calls it, 'for tearing my own repute to tatters'—that the confession, like a modern Rousseau's, would be transformed into a virtue. Here the admitted theatricality comes perilously close to exhibitionism, the impulse to 'glory in the feminine aspects of my character' too much indulged in to make unembarrassed reading. Yet there is much to be said on the other side. Autobiography is a loose form of literature and can survive treatment that would be fatal elsewhere. To digress, to turn aside as a thought strikes one—as the memory of the American negro struck Powys while summing up his impressions of the United States:

> But I have not yet touched upon the most important blessing in this nomadic life of mine . . . I found myself in contact with a race of human beings who are as superior to the rest of humanity, in all the qualities that I, as a philosopher, have come most to admire, as moss is superior to lichen . . .
>
> Slavery, with its appalling slave-ships navigated by so many sea-dogs of English birth, has at least, this worst crime of our race, resulted in the emergence of a divine and incomparable breed of men and women . . . How this black race did redeem humanity for me as I moved about their adopted home! . . . I came to look forward to every 'Diner' because of its African waiter and to every night-coach because of its African porter. The mere sound of these people's voices . . .

—such digressions are no more a weakness here than to be conscious, as John Cowper Powys has always been, of the masks which a complicated, sensitive personality like himself has necessarily had to assume in order to face the world. The overall impression left by the *Autobiography* is one of respect for a soul seeking to come to terms with itself, if we can also see why the paradoxes in the author's nature have so irritated some of his closest friends.

He was affectionately caricatured as 'Jack Welsh' in Louis Wilkinson's novel *The Buffoon*, and in *Blasphemy and Religion* (1916) Wilkinson contrasted the 'sensationalism' of *Wood and Stone* with the 'valid experience' of Theodore's *Soliloquies of a Hermit*, maintaining that while John Cowper's novel is 'as sounding brass and tinkling cymbal', people would still be reading the *Soliloquies* in a hundred years' time. This is an over-kind judgement on the *Soliloquies* themselves, if an impressive forecast—made before most of them were written—of the abiding quality of Theodore's novels and stories. There is certainly a relevant distinction, in point of 'valid experience', between the best novels and stories of Theodore and the early romances of John. But 'sensationalism' is hardly the final word for John Cowper's fiction in its most striking development—as seen, for example, in *Wolf Solent* (1929), *A Glastonbury Romance* (1933), *Jobber Skald* (1935) and *Maiden Castle* (1936). Rather are we conscious, in these extraordinary—but also extraordinarily interesting—productions of the romantic, philosophical and humorous imagination, of a similar blend of strength and weakness to that we observed in the critical work and in the *Autobiography*. For most people's tastes, there is altogether too much talk of such metaphysical sensations as 'The Unpardonable Sin', as in the chapter of that name in the *Glastonbury Romance:*

> The three men had reached the Abbey Barn at the corner of Bere Lane when things came to the worst with Mr. Evans.
> The wild and desperate thought seized him . . . 'Why not fling away every scruple?'

His mind seemed at that second absolutely balanced on a taut and twanging wire between two terrible eternities, an eternity of wilful horror, and an eternity of bleached, arid futility, devoid of all life-sap. He could feel the path to the horror, shivering with deadly phosphorescent sweetness. He could feel the path to the renunciation filling his nostrils with acrid dust, parching his naked feet, withering every human sensation till it was hollow as the shard of a dead beetle! The nature of his temptation was such that it had nothing to redeem it. Such abominable wickedness came straight out of the evil in the heart of the First Cause, travelled through the interlunar spaces, and entered the particular nerve in the erotic organism of Mr. Evans which was predestined to respond to it.

For most people's tastes, too, there are altogether too many exclamation marks on nearly every page of these romances. The true value of an exclamation mark surely becomes weakened if it is placed almost automatically at the end of nearly every sentence, as it frequently is in *Wolf Solent*:

> The intense reality of Mr. Malakite's figure beneath those bed-clothes, of his beard above them, of his nostrils, his old-man's eyelids, his ugly beast-ears, narrowed the reality of his own life, with its gathered memories, into something as concrete, tangible, compact as the bony knuckles of his own gaunt hands now resting upon his protruding knees! Thought? It was 'thought', of course! But not thought in the abstract. It was the thought of a tree, of a snake, of an ox, of a man, a man begotten, a man conceived, a man like enough to die to-morrow! With what within him had he felt that shrewd thrust just now about his true-love Chris? Not with any 'glassy essence'. Simply with his vegetable-animal integrity, *with his life*, as a tree would feel the loss of its companion . . . as a beast the loss of its mate!

This breathless, feminine, introspective prose is typical of many chapters in the romances, as it is of many passages in the *Autobiography* and in the critical and philosophical works. But it has its more admirable side. Novelists who are as much interested in the darker and more eccentric 'countries of the mind' as in the normal actions and thoughts of their characters are not common in English literature; to find a parallel we must turn rather to some of the Russian novelists of the nineteenth century, particularly perhaps to Dostoievsky, whom Powys regards 'with Thomas Hardy and Sir Walter Scott as his sole rivals, as the greatest of all novelists in the world.' John Cowper's protean nature serves him well in the romances: the 'masks' and the 'feminine aspects' are here given a local habitation and a name—the locality being mainly the Somerset and Dorset of his own upbringing, the name being Wolf Solent, Christie Malakite, John Crow, Nell Zoyland, 'Bloody Johnny', Owen Evans or another. Every character shares in John Cowper's own introspective habits, even in the most private and intimate circumstances of life:

> And now, as their dalliance sank into quiescence, one of Wolf's final thoughts before he slept was of the vast tracts of unknown country that every human consciousness includes in its scope. Here, to the superficial eye, were two skulls, lying side by side; but, in reality, here were two far-extending continents, each with its own sky, its own land and water, its own strange-blowing winds. And it was only because his own soul had been, so to speak, washed clean of its body that day that he was able to feel as he felt at this moment. But—even so—what those thoughts of hers had been, that he had interrupted by his return, he knew no better now than when first he had entered her room and had blown out her candle.

When John Cowper's genuine insights are balanced against his 'sensationalism' it must be admitted that he has explored more than most novelists into those 'vast tracts of unknown country' which have always so fascinated him— even if, in the final analysis, he has only discovered himself. His most famous novel, *A Glastonbury Romance*, which is a modern interpretation or endorsement of the ancient legend about Joseph of Arimathaea and the Holy Grail:

> . . . what really allured me about the Holy Grail were the unholy elements in both its history and its mystery . . . the unquestionable fact that it was much older than Christianity itself . . .

even this novel, with its thousand pages and scores of
individual characters, is no real exception to the general
characteristic governing all Powys's work. 'Every face on
the canvas', John Redwood Anderson has truly written, is
'an aspect of a multitudinous and all-embracing self-
portrait.' Or, as John Cowper has himself put it, in a recent
edition of an earlier novel: 'Writing a preface to this book
entitled *Wolf Solent* is like writing a commentary on my
whole life . . .'

Llewelyn Powys was at times John Cowper's severest
critic—once accusing him of being 'spiritually insincere'—
but to this brother, twelve years younger, 'Daddy Jack'
was the supreme genius of the family, 'by far the most
exciting and God-like figure I have ever had to do with'.
He felt he owed nearly everything to his brother's stimulating talk and encouragement:

> Have I not for a quarter of a century [he wrote in 1926] followed
> in the wake of John Cowper? All that I am I owe to him. Like a
> sagacious Sancho Panza, I have ever kept close behind his great
> medieval wain full of the foison of I know not what rich harvest-
> field. And whatever out of its largess his ample wagon gave to the
> wayside hedge, that have I had the wit to garner and . . . carry
> shrewdly off to the nearest market. For let them say what they will,
> it is John alone of all of us who can be likened to the forked
> lightning, he alone has undisputed access to those deep, cool wells
> where the gods themselves let down their buckets.

The comparison of John Cowper to Don Quixote has
an unintentional critical force, but Llewelyn was too modest
in calling himself the Sancho Panza. To his brother's
encouragement he certainly owed a good deal, and his work
in general can be described as 'autobiography' with even
greater truth than John Cowper's. To John's influence, too,
can be traced those features of Llewelyn's prose style which
their brother, the architect A. R. Powys, rightly called
'affected'. There is hardly an unusual word in the whole
of Theodore's writings: 'unclay' in the novel of that name

is the only instance that springs to mind. But both John
Cowper and Llewelyn Powys, like their elder contemporary
Frederick Rolfe ('Baron Corvo'), are very fond of the
unusual, particularly the archaic, word. As John Cowper's
romances are full of words like 'mal-ease', 'malcontent',
'deviltry', 'discomfortable', 'umbrageous', 'talismanic', 'wit-
tol', 'pilgarlic', 'welkin', 'ichor', 'semi-cirque' and 'eidolon',
so Llewelyn is fond of 'whoreson', 'benison', 'shotten',
'largess', 'foison' and 'wain'.

But when Llewelyn Powys was not trying to 'write
choice periods of prose', as he himself put it, he could
write as simply and effectively as Theodore. His gift for
fiction was not great, compared with his brothers'; he
lacked John's fertility of invention and Theodore's power
for allegory and fable. His one real novel, *Apples Be Ripe*
(1930), for all the charm of its best passages, is a lesser
thing altogether than his 'imaginary autobiography' *Love
and Death* (1939) and the half-fictional, half-reminiscent
stories and sketches in *Ebony and Ivory* and *Black Laughter*.
Where Llewelyn excels is in his evocative descriptions of
place and of nature: the Palestine of *A Pagan's Pilgrimage*
(1931), the England of *Earth Memories* (1934), the Africa of
Black Laughter:

> And then darkness would fall and the air would become full of
> unexplained noises and strange unexpected smells, and the African
> wind would blow against our faces and set the long tufted branches
> of the forest trees tossing against each other, and we would stumble
> through the grass to the old familiar shamba-track and so come
> nearer and nearer to the small lamp-lit house, where . . . we would
> sit over a crackling wood fire and talk of old days in Somerset-
> shire . . .
>
> Suddenly clear and unmistakable out of the darkness would come
> the heavy booming of a gun. I never heard one of those gun-traps
> go off without a curious shock. One felt as though oneself was
> present down there under the trees by the black flowing water in
> utter loneliness . . .
>
> Morning would come at last, and we would . . . set off through
> the damp scrub down to the trap, and . . . there before us, stretched

out upon the cool, shining, dewy grass, would lie the long snake-like body of a gilded ebon-spotted cat. The mere fact that such an animal should actually be abroad upon the earth used to seem to me amazing . . . What taut muscles! What a suggestion of lithe and dangerous strength knit together with elastic ligaments! And how heavy that limp skin was, that limp gorgeous skin that smelt of the fierce leopard sweat of a thousand jungle nights.

Llewelyn Powys travelled nearly as widely as D. H. Lawrence. Italy, Greece, Palestine, Kenya, the United States, the West Indies . . . were among the countries he saw and described so vividly in his books and letters. And a walk on the Dorset downs with Llewelyn Powys was as fruitful an experience for his companions as a walk with Lawrence through the Midland countryside. Both men had the same gift for seeing nature with fresh eyes, with the added intensity of vision that has so often been remarked of consumptives.

It was in Kenya that he first found himself as a writer, and *Ebony and Ivory* (begun in England in 1913) and *Black Laughter* remain two of the best of his books. They also gave him his first welcome taste of success, so much so indeed that John Cowper in the *Autobiography* reflects—wryly as a writer, proudly as a brother—that in the middle twenties Llewelyn's reputation in the United States as much surpassed his own as Theodore's did in England: 'They were both recognized authors while I was still "John, the Talker".' It was not till the publication of the *Glastonbury Romance* and the *Autobiography* in the thirties that the fame of 'Don John' exceeded that of the self-styled Sancho Panza.

III

T. F. POWYS: THE EARLY WORKS

Few writers of our time have had so outwardly uneventful a life as Theodore Francis Powys. Born, like his elder brothers John and Littleton, at Shirley in Derbyshire, in 1875, he did not follow them to Cambridge but after his schooldays became a farmer for a short while in Suffolk. Then, in the autumn of 1901, he moved to a labourer's cottage in the seaside village of Studland, Dorset, resolving to live a life of contemplation on his father's allowance of £60 a year. He left Studland for East Chaldon in 1904, and it was about this time that he began to write *An Interpretation of Genesis*, privately printed in 1908. He started his first novel, *Mr. Tasker's Gods*, in 1916, but he did not begin to be known till 1923, with the publication of *The Left Leg*. Thereafter his publication was constant till the early thirties, after which he wrote little of importance. He moved in 1940 to Mappowder, where he died in 1953.

He was late in finding his true path, but then comparatively prolific for about ten years, from 1921 to 1931. He blossomed in the late summer or early autumn of his life, his best work being accomplished in his late forties and fifties. But we must always bear in mind, when speaking of T. F. Powys, the often considerable gap between composition and publication. As his son has told us:

> For many years publishers and editors would have none of him, and he worked on without recognition. His cupboards became filled with manuscripts copied and recopied laboriously in long-hand. When finally he became known his books were published in quick succession, for he only needed to open one of those cup-boards to produce a ready-made novel or a short story.

I shall treat of his early work in order of composition, the order being known in most cases on the authority of Powys himself; otherwise his progress towards mastery would appear haphazard.

The *Interpretation of Genesis* need not detain us. There is little in this dialogue between Moses the Lawgiver and the author's mouthpiece, Zetetes the Seeker, to suggest the great Powys of *Mr. Weston* and the *Fables*, unless we see a faint resemblance to the latter in the use of the dialogue

form. *Soliloquies of a Hermit* (written 1915, published 1916)
is much more interesting, for here we first come across
some of his leading ideas. For Powys, death is the desired
end; and it would appear from the *Soliloquies* that he was
led to this glad acceptance by considering that the most
beautiful things in life blossom and fade, while unlovely
things, like the stones of the field and 'the everlasting mud',
remain. 'The attributes of immortality' to Powys are
'greed, hardness of heart, cunning—all the biting instincts
of the animal.' His reverence for Jesus stems from his
appreciation of the way Christ preached and practised the
opposite. 'It does not matter if He is true', he adds: 'He is
beyond all Truth.' The *Soliloquies* are lay sermons; the
clerical inheritance, though brought here to a most unortho-
dox pass, was not entirely revoked.

More important, from the point of view of Powys the
literary artist, is the way this early book of sometimes
undigested philosophy looks forward to his greater work.
We see, for instance, the *Fables* in embryo when he con-
fesses here that he wants:

> to cultivate the kind of mind that can turn . . . a dull hour into
> heavenly glory . . . For what we call dullness is really the best soil
> we can dig in, because the gold that it yields is very precious . . .

Powys, however, had some way to go before he could
mine gold from the seemingly dull and ordinary things in
life; and he was always liable to fall into his main weakness of
whimsicality, which makes some of his work 'very precious'
in a different sense. To begin with, he was not quite sure
of his path, and—curious as it seems for the future author
of *Mr. Weston* and *Unclay*—he started his career in fiction
by trying to be a realistic novelist. Between the composition
of the *Soliloquies* and their publication in England (they were
published first in the United States through the recommenda-
tion of John Cowper) he wrote two novels—*Mr. Tasker's
Gods* (1916-17, published 1924) and *Black Bryony* (1917,
published 1923)—besides a *nouvelle*, *Hester Dominy*, and a

number of short stories. There are some fine things in all
these, but their most striking characteristic, compared with
the majority of the later work, is their bitter irony, their
refusal to find comfort or compensation. *Mr. Tasker* has
ironic moments worthy of Swift, but in general—and the
criticism is almost equally true of *Black Bryony* and *Hester*—
the worldly characters like Tasker himself (whose 'gods'
are his pigs) have it so much their own way, and the
unworldly are so feeble and so clearly doomed to failure
from the start, that the novel leaves an unbalanced impression. Powys at this period (which was also, of course, the
period of the bloodiest fighting of the First World War) seems
to have been so bitterly convinced of man's inhumanity to
man that his feelings would not allow him the artistic
freedom he desired. There is a parallel here with his
eighteenth-century ancestor Cowper, whose poetry he so
much admired.

The change comes with *The Left Leg*: written 1921,
published 1923. Like another Christian, though an heretical
one, Powys passed through the Slough of Despond and
took at last the true, allegorical path that was to lead to his
most inspiring work. The reference to the *Pilgrim's Progress*
is not inapposite, for from *The Left Leg* onwards Bunyan is
evidently very much in Powys's mind. Eschewing realism,
as usually understood, Powys became an allegorist and a
fabulist and in so doing achieved, in the poetic or dramatic
sense, a more profound reality. The worldly and the vicious
prosper in *The Left Leg* almost as much as in *Mr. Tasker*,
and the innocents in Madder village come to grief; but a
whole new dimension is introduced, symbolised by the
travelling tinker Jar. 'Who be wold Jar?' Mad Tom Button
asks, and he answers his own question:

> ' 'E be the leaf that do drift in the wind. 'E be the cloud that do
> cross the moon at night time. 'E be the stone that a poor man do
> take up in road to throw at 'is dog. 'E be the pond weeds where do
> bide the wold toad. 'E be the bastard child before 'tis born. Wold
> Jar be come.'

And with the coming of 'wold Jar', both to Madder village and to Powys's work, the road to *Mr. Weston*, the *Fables* and *Unclay* lies open. The name Jar probably comes from the Hebrew divine name YHWH, translated into English as Jahweh or Jehovah. But Powys's God is a pantheistic conception, whether symbolised by Tinker Jar, by Squire Jar in *The Key of the Field*, by the fisherman in *Mockery Gap*, by Mr. Weston in the *Good Wine* or by the vision of Christ the compassionate which appears to the good dog in the fable *The Dog and the Lantern:*

> 'The Saviour of the world', replied the Christ, 'can be everything. Little Betty may find a lucky stone by the seaside—that stone am I. Dig down into the clay where poor Tom, the madman, lies buried. His coffin-boards are rotted, his flesh is clay—I am he. The sexton stole the church oil—I was that too—and sold it to the shepherd, who filled me with it.'

Absolute consistency in philosophical ideas is not required of a novelist or a poet. It may be doubted, for example, whether Powys's idea of the grave as a place of rest is quite consistent with his denial of immortality. We only know we have been asleep when we wake up, and if we do not wake up the whole analogy of death with sleeping is logically false. It is a fair criticism of Powys to point out, too, that sometimes his Gods are too numerous for conviction: there does not seem to be any necessity for bringing Jar into *Mr. Weston* or Mr. Weston into *Unclay*. But what is important is the undoubted fact that, with this whole new dimension added, the novels and stories become much more alive. There is a poetic reality in *The Left Leg* more impressive, on the whole, than the comparatively laboured realism of *Mr. Tasker*, *Black Bryony* or *Hester Dominy*. Farmer Mew, who 'do swallow all', is not a realistic figure, but he is a convincing personification of greed, a worthy adversary for Tinker Jar:

> The figure and the aspect of the man were terrible. He stood as though he were resisting to the uttermost a huge force. With every sinew he fought Jar.

He is as real to the reader as comparable characters in the plays of Ben Jonson and the novels of Dickens.

The success of *The Left Leg* must have shown Powys where his true strength lay, though for some time he was to dissipate it by his unfortunate taste for the fanciful. The succeeding novels of the early twenties—*Mark Only* (1922, published 1924) *Mockery Gap* (1923, published 1925) and *Innocent Birds* (1923-4, published 1926)—show a progressive mastery in control of the allegorical, the last-named in particular being one of Powys's most impressive early achievements. Dorset in these novels, like the Yorkshire moors in *Wuthering Heights*, is the world in miniature: 'a picture', as Mr. Solly puts it in *Innocent Birds*, 'that can show a vaster and a grander one behind it.' If Powys had ended his career here, however, he would not have been the great writer he so clearly is, for even the best of these early novels and stories can fairly be criticized for their weaknesses of whimsicality and melodrama. But the first masterpiece lay immediately ahead. Powys began *Mr. Weston's Good Wine* in January 1924 and completed it in the autumn of the following year; it was published in 1927 and has been the most widely read and the most frequently translated of all his work.

IV

MR. WESTON AND AFTER

The difference between *Mr. Weston's Good Wine* and the best of the early novels and stories is not one of kind—not the difference that separates *The Left Leg* from *Mr. Tasker's Gods*—but one of degree: this first masterpiece, completed when the author was fifty, is a triumph of tone and controlled energy, in which the incidental weaknesses of even the best of the early work are almost entirely overcome. It makes deceptively easy reading, but behind the apparent simplicity lay eighteen months' writing and rewriting, before the

author was satisfied that he had the precise effect he desired.
Mr. Weston himself is a creation who could easily have
become spoilt for the reader at many delicate points,
particularly in the early chapters. We can only admire the
way Powys has succeeded in making the wine-merchant
human and likeable and at the same time indubitably God,
the creator of the village of Folly Down (there is an actual
village of Folly, near Mappowder) and the town of
Maidenbridge (Dorchester) which Hardy in the Wessex
novels calls Casterbridge. Mr. Weston can move easily from
the most familiar speech and all too human failings—he
has an author's vanity about his own collected writings,
the Bible—to the most profound and lofty utterance; he
can discuss the poet Cowper with Luke Bird and also, like
Jesus at Cana, turn the water into wine to facilitate Luke's
marriage to Jenny Bunce; he can converse on equal and
waggish terms with the landlord and customers of the
Angel Inn, but when he hides his face in his mug and takes
'a very deep draught' the words (from *Isaiah* XLV, 7):

> 'I form the light, and create darkness: I make peace, and create
> evil: I, the Lord, do all these things . . .'

are heard by everyone in the room, though no one knows
who said them. The triumph of the novel is partly a triumph
of language.

Dorset is the epitome of the world, and the Dorset dialect
is transformed into poetry without losing its characteristic
local qualities. As early as *The Left Leg* Powys had been
able to make this transformation; here it is the grave-digger
Mr. Grunter who rises to the heights of simple eloquence
when Mr. Weston confronts the Mumby brothers with
the corrupted body of Ada Kiddle, who had drowned
herself after being ravished by them:

> Though the worms had destroyed Ada's beauty, her shape was
> still there, and Mr. Grunter regarded her compassionately . . .
> 'When life bain't', said Mr. Grunter slowly, 'death be' . . .

A picture may move a man, and this picture affected Mr.
Grunter . . . 'Ada', he said . . .' 'tain't I that have moulded 'ee,
'tain't I that have rotted thee's merry ways wi' wormy clay . . .'
    . . . Mr. Weston had covered his face with his hands, as if he
wept.

God as a tradesman, with a Ford car: it is an even more
original conception than God as a travelling tinker, whose
'only garment is a thundercloud but he sometimes mends
kettles'. Mr. Weston sells two kinds of wine: the Light
Wine, which is Love, and for which the payment is Love
returned; and the Dark Wine, which is Death, and for
which the payment is Life. And these two wines, in the
Powysian creed, are not two wines but one wine—an idea
which Powys developed further in *Unclay*, where Death
says to Priscilla Hayhoe:

> 'I kill, and Love gives life, but in reality we are one and the same.
> We often exchange our weapons. And then 'tis I that give life,
> and Love that kills . . .'

as Love kills Tamar in *Mr. Weston* after she has met her
angel Michael 'in oak-tree bed'.

Another subtle point in *Mr. Weston*, that the wine-
merchant himself longs to die but cannot—'I long to drink
my own dark wine'—is developed further, not only in
Unclay but in *The Only Penitent* and the *Fables*. This latter
series of stories—written 1927, published 1929, republished
1934 under the title *No Painted Plumage*—is Powys's second
masterpiece, as original in conception and as successful in
execution as *Mr. Weston* itself. It owes part of its origin to a
remark by Llewelyn Powys, who suggested to his brother
that he should 'write about *anything*; write about that log
of wood and that old boot.' Somewhat in the spirit of their
ancestor Cowper's *Task*, Powys proceeded to do just that, in
a series of stories whose principal feature is dialogue between
such varied personalities as a clout and a pan, a donkey and
a rabbit, a stone and a skull, a bucket and a rope, a spittoon

and a slate. These stories—delightfully humorous and ironic, yet often the vehicle for the profoundest meditations upon life and death—rival *Mr. Weston* itself in their masterly simplicity, in their easy transition from the most familiar, everyday things to the most momentous. In the opening fable, for instance, the pan passes from talk of Mrs. Keddle's cracked bedroom basin to remark:

> 'Time goes on—'
> 'Alas! that is true,' murmured the clout, 'and I that am but a cotton rag, and all the Keddles upon the earth, together with the most huge and distant stars, must know of its going.'

The Dorset dialect is again transformed into poetry, as when the church clerk in the fable *Mr. Pim and the Holy Crumb* imagines God to resemble the landlord at the village inn:

> ' 'E did draw I out of 'Is great barrel into a little cup, and when I die 'E do but empty I again into the dirt from whence I came. They be 'Is notions . . . Some do fall of a sudden, some bent and tottering like wold Barker do tarry long, but all do go to dust.'

It is in this fable—perhaps the masterpiece of the whole series—that the Holy Crumb, dropped by Mr. Pim at his first Communion, repeats the lonely cry of Mr. Weston the wine-trader. 'But bain't 'E God?' demands Mr. Pim, puzzled. 'Yes, alas so!' replies the Crumb. . . . The awful loneliness of God, however many forms He may take in the pantheistic imagination, was a problem that never ceased to exercise Powys's mind.

The chief of the later works, in order of publication (the exact time of writing not being known here), are *Kindness in a Corner* (1930), a light, humorous novel with one magnificent chapter about a country churchyard entitled 'The Dirt of God'; the story *The Only Penitent* (1931), later included in the collection *Bottle's Path* (1946); his last full-length novel *Unclay* (1931); and the *nouvelle*, *The Two Thieves*, published with two other stories in

1932. Powys had written stories of varying length, collected at different times, from as early as 1917; and he continued to do so. At his best, he is equal to the most distinguished writers of the short story in our time; but it must be admitted that there are quite a number of his shorter pieces which are very feeble indeed in their forced whimsicality and stale repetition of effects.

His last full-length novel, *Unclay*, was a conscious attempt to sum up his life's work. He had always been fond of giving his characters in one story a new lease of life in another; such figures as Luke Bird, Miss Pettifer, Mr. Balliboy, Lord Bullman, 'wold Barker', Farmer Told . . . recur frequently. But the way characters and situations from earlier novels recur in *Unclay* is evidence of deliberate design. He could not resurrect Farmer Mew, because that personification of greed had blown himself up, his left leg falling from the sky 'according to the scriptures' of the English nursery rhyme; but the brutal Farmer Mere in *Unclay* is a deliberate reminder of him, as is Mere's victim Susie Dawe of Mew's victim Mary Gillet. Powys even goes back to the mood of the *Soliloquies*, for the meditations which are a feature of this last novel:

> In the common lives of people, one power is always waiting ready to drive out another, in order to rule in its place. There is always a stronger one coming. Each guardian of the temple is slain in his turn, then the victor becomes priest in his stead. Power that conquers power is the order of all our lives, but who is it that dare name the last power to kill? What will He do, when the fatal blow is struck, and He becomes lord of the temple, with no rival to challenge His victory? . . . Shall He hear again the many trampling feet of a new generation of men, or will the last enemy destroy Him too? Will God die? . . .
>
> All thought in Dodder was quieted. Still waters covered all motion, and no mental webs were being spun there that bring false hope to man. To grow like the field flowers, what else could man do? To bloom in the summer . . . and drink the dark wine of the sadness of the earth during the fall. To breathe deep again,

perhaps, when the winter's sleep is ended . . . To exist as a creature
of the earth for a moment, what more should be needed?

The evening gnats quivered and danced in the warm air, unmind-
ful of danger. The swallows caught them and they heeded not the
act . . . So the evening is devoured by the night, and the dawn by
the day.

Unclay is the complement to *Mr. Weston*: as time stops
in that novel, so here Death loses his commission and is
forced to give his scythe a rest. And Powys here tries to
solve some of the philosophical problems raised by the
earlier masterpiece. The attempt is not entirely successful;
and while this last novel is Powys's most profound treatment of the themes of Love and Death, it is not so much of
an artistic unity as *Mr. Weston*.

The Only Penitent, written about the same time as *Unclay*,
sums up Powys's matured views in a smaller space. No one
comes to Mr. Hayhoe to confess his sins till one sultry
afternoon, culminating in a thunderstorm—the Powyses use
weather for dramatic effect with Shakespearean assurance—
a Person descends Madder Hill, enters the church, and
kneels humbly before him:

'Who are you?' asked Mr. Hayhoe, whose own voice sounded
strange to him.

'I am the Only Penitent', replied Jar. 'I have come to confess my
sin to you . . . Only by the forgiveness of man can I be saved . . .
By love, all is forgiven.'

'Dare I love you?' asked Mr. Hayhoe.

Jar bowed his head.

'I crucified my son', he said . . . ' 'Twas I who created every
terror in the earth, the rack, the plague, all despair, all torment . . .
Can you love me now?'

In earlier days, Powys would have had no answer; even
Mr. Weston is silent when accused by Martin Mumby at
the graveside of Ada Kiddle. But now, in an inspired
moment, Mr. Hayhoe looks up from the kneeling Jar and
sees his wife Priscilla waiting for him; and he knows that

Jar's bitterness—like the bitterness of *Mr. Tasker's Gods* and *Black Bryony*—is not the whole truth:

> 'You have not told all', he said. 'You have not spoken of the joy and love that a woman can give, you have not told of the great peace that you also can bestow upon those who desire it . . .'
>
> 'I destroy all men with a sword', said Jar. 'I cast them down into the pit, they become nothing.'
>
> 'Hold!' cried Mr. Hayhoe. 'Is that last word true?'
>
> 'It is', answered Jar.
>
> 'Then, in the name of Man,' said Mr. Hayhoe boldly, 'I forgive your sin; I pardon and deliver you from all your evil; confirm and strengthen you in all goodness, and bring you to everlasting death.'

Jar is forgiven by his creation; Mr. Weston can drink his own dark wine. . . . There is a perfection about the ending of this story that is not common in English literature. It did not come easily; all the bitter irony of *Mr. Tasker* and its successors had to be worked through first, the blind alleys of whimsicality had to be thoroughly explored, before Powys could attain these apparently simple heights. He was not often to attain them again, though *The Two Thieves* is a fine and assured allegory, in which John Roe—or Everyman—occupies much the same position in regard to Tinker Jar as Mr. Hayhoe in *The Only Penitent*.

V

CONCLUSION

It is an axiom in literary criticism that an author shall be judged by his best works, and fortunately in the case of the Powys brothers there has been little controversy as to which these are. The greatness of T. F. Powys is clearly in his *Fables* and in the more allegorical of his novels and stories, particularly perhaps *Mr. Weston's Good Wine, Unclay, The Left Leg, The Only Penitent* and *The Two Thieves*. Where he has attempted a more realistic path, as in *Mr. Tasker's Gods* and *Black Bryony*, or where his weakness for the whimsical has got the better of him, as in *Kindness in a Corner* and some of the shorter stories, he is not, on the whole, so convincing and cannot be called more than an interesting minor writer of our time.

Similarly, though John Cowper Powys has written a good deal in nearly every branch of literature except—curiously enough—the dramatic, he is clearly not one of our greater poets or our greater poet-critics. The 'poetry' of this most Celtic—even at times most 'wild and woolly Western'—of the Powys brothers is rather to be found in his *Autobiography* and in what he has himself well described as 'the sort of mystic-humorous, Pantagruelian, Shandean, Quixotic Romance' that is seen at its best in the novel whose 'heroine is the Grail'. *A Glastonbury Romance* has never been everyone's reading; it requires for its appreciation, not only sympathy with the idiom of its author, but a series of suspensions of disbelief that are by no means easy to sustain in the twentieth century. In spite of its popular and humorous aspects—John Cowper's superlative opinion of Theodore's more ironic humour is a compliment that can sometimes be repaid to his own—it is clearly a work destined to be fully enjoyed only by scholars.

Llewelyn Powys has two styles of writing, which appeal to two distinct publics—or to two generations. His more allusive and affected style is reminiscent of the Lamb-Hazlitt circle as known to us through their essays; his biographer Malcolm Elwin says truly that he 'may eventually claim his place as a prose-writer in the dynasty of Landor and Pater'. But there is another Llewelyn, of a plainer style, who appeals more to the taste of the mid-twentieth century. In some of the chapters of *Black Laughter* the very feel of Africa is given to us in a relatively unadorned prose that is the reverse of Lamb's or Pater's and whose nearest modern equivalent is George Orwell's.

The first public critic of the Powys brothers was their

friend Louis Wilkinson, and after the lapse of nearly half
a century it must be admitted that Mr. Wilkinson's early
judgement has been proved right. The classic of the family,
one can but agree, is T. F. Powys, though not by any means in
the whole of his work nor to the detriment of his brothers.
Theodore's subject is often Man rather than men and women;
in their treatment of individuals, John Cowper and Llewelyn
are sometimes superior. Where Theodore gives the type,
they give the personality: the old sexton in *Love and Death*,
for instance, compared with old Sextonhood in the *Fables*.

The Powys brothers—all three 'poets' in the widest sense
of the word, though their poetic, religious view of life has
mostly been expressed in prose—present a somewhat
isolated picture in the English literature of the twentieth
century. Belonging to no current school or contemporary
trend, they have never been widely popular, never been
honoured with Nobel Prizes or Orders of Merit, and at
different times have been rashly dismissed as old-fashioned.
In the Marxist hey-day of the thirties, their concern with
ultimate problems seemed bourgeois; and when ultimate
problems—or ultimate answers—became the rage in the
forties, the heretical Powyses were swept aside in the flood
of an orthodox Christian revival. Their insistence on the
brutal as well as the peaceful aspects of country life removed
them from the 'culture-agriculture' equation of contemporary back-to-the-land theorists, as their Rabelaisian
delight in what Shakespeare called 'country matters' from
the more urban and cosmopolitan varieties of the erotic.
But writers who have never been in fashion cannot logically
be accused of becoming out of it.

THE POWYS FAMILY

A Select Bibliography

(Place of publication London unless stated otherwise)

JOHN COWPER POWYS

Bibliography:

A BIBLIOGRAPHY OF THE FIRST EDITIONS OF JOHN COWPER POWYS, by
L. E. Siberell. Cincinnati (1934).

Separate Works:

ODES AND OTHER POEMS (1896).

POEMS (1899).

THE WAR AND CULTURE. New York (1914). *Polemic*
—English edition, entitled *The Menace of German Culture*, 1915.

VISIONS AND REVISIONS. New York (1915). *Criticism*
—revised edition with new preface by the author, 1955.

WOOD AND STONE. New York (1915). *Novel*
—English edition, 1917.

CONFESSIONS OF TWO BROTHERS. Rochester, N.Y. (1916). *Autobiography*
—with Llewelyn Powys.

WOLF'S BANE RHYMES. New York (1916). *Verse*

ONE HUNDRED BEST BOOKS. New York (1916). *Commentary*

RODMOOR. New York (1916). *Novel*

SUSPENDED JUDGMENTS. New York (1916). *Criticism*

MANDRAGORA. New York (1917). *Verse*

THE COMPLEX VISION. New York (1920). *Philosophy*

SAMPHIRE. New York (1922). *Verse*

PSYCHOANALYSIS AND MORALITY. San Francisco (1923). *Philosophy*

THE ART OF HAPPINESS. Girard, Kansas (1925). *Philosophy*

THE RELIGION OF A SCEPTIC. New York (1925). *Philosophy*

DUCDAME (1925). *Novel*

THE SECRET OF SELF-DEVELOPMENT. Girard, Kansas (1926.) *Philosophy*

ESSAYS ON MONTAIGNE, PASCAL, VOLTAIRE. Girard, Kansas (c.1926).
Criticism

THE ART OF FORGETTING THE UNPLEASANT. Girard, Kansas (1928).
Philosophy

WOLF SOLENT (1929). *Novel*
—new edition with preface by the author, 1961.

THE MEANING OF CULTURE. New York (1929). *Philosophy*
—English edition, 1930. New edition with new introduction by the
author, 1939.

IN DEFENCE OF SENSUALITY (1930). *Philosophy*

THE OWL, THE DUCK, AND—MISS ROWE! MISS ROWE! Chicago (1930).
Short stories

DEBATE! IS MODERN MARRIAGE A FAILURE? New York (1930.) *Polemic*
—with Bertrand Russell.

DOROTHY M. RICHARDSON (1931). *Criticism*

A GLASTONBURY ROMANCE. New York (1932). *Novel*
—English edition, 1933. New edition with preface by the author,
1955.

A PHILOSOPHY OF SOLITUDE (1933). *Philosophy*
—American and English editions have different prefaces.

WEYMOUTH SANDS. New York (1934). *Novel*
—English edition (with modified text) entitled *Jobber Skald*, 1935.

AUTOBIOGRAPHY (1934).

THE ART OF HAPPINESS (1935). *Philosophy*
—not identical with American pamphlet with the same title.

MAIDEN CASTLE. New York (1936). *Novel*
—English edition, 1937.

MORWYN (1937). *Novel*

THE PLEASURES OF LITERATURE (1938). *Essays*

OWEN GLENDOWER. New York (1940). *Novel*
—English edition, 1941.

MORTAL STRIFE (1941). *Commentary*

THE ART OF GROWING OLD (1944). *Philosophy*

DOSTOIEVSKY (1946). *Criticism*

PAIR DADENI or THE CAULDRON OF REBIRTH. Carmarthen (1946).
  Pamphlet

OBSTINATE CYMRIC: ESSAYS 1935-1947. Carmarthen (1947). *Criticism*

RABELAIS (1948). *Biography*
—with new translations and critical commentary.

PORIUS (1951). *Novel*

THE INMATES (1952). *Novel*

IN SPITE OF (1953). *Philosophy*

ATLANTIS (1954). *Novel*

THE BRAZEN HEAD (1956). *Novel*

LUCIFER (1956). *Verse*

UP AND OUT (1957). *Stories*
—contains also 'the Mountains of the Moon'.

THE LETTERS OF JOHN COWPER POWYS TO LOUIS WILKINSON: 1935-1956
  (1958)
—edited by L. Wilkinson.

HOMER AND THE AETHER (1959). *Paraphrase of 'The Iliad'.*

ALL OR NOTHING (1960). *Novel*

Note: J. C. Powys's introductions to books by other writers have
  been omitted from this check-list.

LLEWELYN POWYS

Separate Works:

EBONY AND IVORY (1923). *Stories and Sketches*
—with a preface by E. Shanks. American edition has a preface by
  T. Dreiser.

THIRTEEN WORTHIES. New York (1923). *Biographical Essays*
—English edition, 1924, with preface by Van W. Brooks.

HONEY AND GALL. Girard, Kansas (1924). *Essays*

CUP-BEARERS OF WINE AND HELLEBORE. Girard, Kansas (1924). *Literary
  Studies*

BLACK LAUGHTER. New York (1924). *Stories and Sketches*
—English edition, 1925. New edition with foreword by N. Farson,
1953.

SKIN FOR SKIN. New York (1925). *Autobiography*
—English edition, 1926.

THE VERDICT OF BRIDLEGOOSE. New York (1926). *Autobiography*
—English edition, 1927. This was reprinted in one volume with
Skin for Skin, 1948.

HENRY HUDSON (1927). *Biography*

OUT OF THE PAST. Pasadena, California (c.1928). *Essay*
—later included in *Earth Memories*.

THE CRADLE OF GOD (1929). *Philosophy*
—new edition with preface by E. Carr, 1949.

AN HOUR ON CHRISTIANITY. New York (1930). *Philosophy*
—English edition (entitled *The Pathetic Fallacy: A Study of Christianity*),
1930, reprinted in *The Thinker's Library*, 1931.

APPLES BE RIPE (1930). *Novel*
—reprinted in *Big Ben Books*, 1940.

A PAGAN'S PILGRIMAGE (1931). *Travel*

IMPASSIONED CLAY (1931). *Philosophy*

THE LIFE AND TIMES OF ANTHONY A'WOOD (1932)
—abridged from A. Clark's edition with introductory essay. Reprinted in *World's Classics*, 1961.

NOW THAT THE GODS ARE DEAD. New York (1932). *Philosophy*
—English edition, with *The Glory of Life*, 1949.

GLORY OF LIFE (1934). *Philosophy*
—a *Golden Cockerell Press* limited edition, with wood engravings by
R. Gibbings, 1930.

EARTH MEMORIES (1934). *Essays*
—with woodcuts by G. M. Powys.

DAMNABLE OPINIONS (1935). *Philosophy*

DORSET ESSAYS (1935). *Essays*
—twelve of these were reprinted (New York, 1938), with *Earth
Memories* and introduction by Van W. Brooks.

THE TWELVE MONTHS (1936). *Essays*

SOMERSET ESSAYS (1937). *Essays*
—republished with *Dorset Essays*, 1957, with introduction by J. C. Powys.

RATS IN THE SACRISTY (1937). *Biographical and Critical essays*
—with preface by J. C. Powys and wood engravings by G. M. Powys.

THE BOOK OF DAYS (1937). *Philosophy*
—thoughts selected from the philosophy of Ll. Powys by J. Wallis, with introduction by Ll. Powys.

LOVE AND DEATH: AN IMAGINARY AUTOBIOGRAPHY (1939)
—with introduction by A. Gregory.

A BAKER'S DOZEN. Herrin, Ill. (1939). *Essays*
—with introduction by L. E. Siberell and illustrations by M. Noheimer. English edition, 1941, has introduction by J. C. Powys and decorations by G. M. Powys.

THE LETTERS OF LLEWELYN POWYS (1943)
—selected and edited by L. Wilkinson, with introduction by A. Gregory.

SWISS ESSAYS (1947).

ADVICE TO A YOUNG POET (1949). *Letters*
—to Kenneth Hopkins.

LLEWELYN POWYS: A SELECTION OF HIS WRITINGS (1952)
—selected by K. Hopkins, contains 20 letters first published and 3 essays here first collected.

THEODORE FRANCIS POWYS

Collected Stories:

THE WHITE PATERNOSTER (1930).

BOTTLE'S PATH (1946).

GOD'S EYES A-TWINKLE, selected and introduced by C. Prentice (1947).

Separate Works:

AN INTERPRETATION OF GENESIS (1908). *Meditations*
—privately printed. New edition, 1929.

THE SOLILOQUY OF A HERMIT. New York (1916). *Meditations*
—English edition, 1918, entitled *Soliloquies of a Hermit*.

THE LEFT LEG: HESTER DOMINY: ABRAHAM MEN (1923). *Stories*

BLACK BRYONY (1923). *Novel*
—woodcuts by R. A. Garnett.

MARK ONLY (1924). *Novel*

MR. TASKER'S GODS. New York (1924). *Novel*
—English edition, 1925. (Written 1916-17).

MOCKERY GAP (1925). *Novel*

A STUBBORN TREE (1926). *Story*

INNOCENT BIRDS (1926). *Novel*

FEED MY SWINE (1926). *Story*
—later included in *The White Paternoster*.

A STRONG GIRL and THE BRIDE (1926). *Stories*
—the latter included in *The White Paternoster*.

MR. WESTON'S GOOD WINE (1927). *Novel*
—illustrations by G. Charlton. *Penguin* edition 1937.

THE RIVAL PASTORS (1927). *Story*
—later included in *The White Paternoster*.

WHAT LACK I YET? (1927). *Story*
—later included in *The White Paternoster*.

THE HOUSE WITH THE ECHO (1928). *Stories*
—the title story written 1917-18.

THE DEWPOND (1928).
—later included in *Bottle's Path*.

FABLES (1929)
—new edition, 1934, entitled *No Painted Plumage*.

THE KEY OF THE FIELD (1930). *Story*
—later included in *Bottle's Path*.

URIAH ON THE HILL. Cambridge (1930). *Story*

KINDNESS IN A CORNER (1930). *Novel*

CHRIST IN THE CUPBOARD (1930). *Story*
—later included in *The White Paternoster*.

UNCLE DOTTERY. Bristol (1930). *Story*

WHEN THOU WAST NAKED (1931). *Story*
—later included in *Bottle's Path*.

THE ONLY PENITENT (1931) *Story*
—later included in *Bottle's Path*.

UNCLAY (1931). *Novel*

THE TITHE BARN and THE DOVE AND THE EAGLE (1932). *Stories*
—the latter included in *Bottle's Path*.

THE TWO THIEVES: GOD: IN GOOD EARTH (1932). *Stories*

MAKE THYSELF MANY (1935). *Story*

CAPTAIN PATCH (1935). *Stories*

GOAT GREEN (1937). *Story*
—engravings by G. Morgan. Later included in *Bottle's Path* under the
title of *The Better Gift*.

LITTLETON CHARLES POWYS

THE JOY OF IT (1937). *Memoirs*

THE POWYS FAMILY. Yeovil (1952). *Pamphlet*

STILL THE JOY OF IT (1956). *Memoirs*

ALBERT REGINALD POWYS

THE ENGLISH HOUSE (1929). *Pamphlet*

REPAIR OF ANCIENT BUILDINGS (1929).

THE ENGLISH PARISH CHURCH (1930)
—with an introduction by E. Ferrers.

ORIGINS OF BAD ARCHITECTURE (1931). *Pamphlet*

FROM THE GROUND UP (1937)
—with an introduction by J. C. Powys.

PHILIPPA POWYS

DRIFTWOOD (1930). *Verse*

THE BLACKTHORN WINTER (1930). *Novel*

MARIAN POWYS
LACE AND LACE-MAKING. Boston (1953).

THE POWYS FAMILY
Some Biographical and Critical Studies:

BLASPHEMY AND RELIGION: Dialogue about WOOD AND STONE by
J. C. Powys and THE SOLILOQUY OF A HERMIT by T. F. Powys, by
L. U. Wilkinson. New York (1916).

THE BUFFOON, by L. U. Wilkinson. New York (1916). *Novel*
—contains fictional portrait of J. C. Powys under the name Jack
Welsh.

CRITICAL WOODCUTS, by S. Sherman. New York (1926)
—on Llewelyn Powys, pp. 138-155.

THE NOVELS AND STORIES OF T. F. POWYS, by W. Hunter. Cambridge
(1930).

SWAN'S MILK, by L. Marlow (1934)
—an autobiographical novel which contains many reminiscences of
the Powys Brothers. Marlow is a pen name of L. Wilkinson.

CRUMBS ARE ALSO BREAD, by M. Burrell (1934)
—contains notes on Llewelyn and J. C. Powys, pp. 128-140.

THE POWYS BROTHERS, by R. H. Ward (1936).

WELSH AMBASSADORS, by L. Marlow (1936)
—contains check-list of publications.

GENIUS OF ENGLAND, by H. J. Massingham (1937)
—contains a chapter on Llewelyn Powys.

JOHN COWPER POWYS, by W. C. Derry. Boston (1938)
—an interpretation.

THE TERRIBLE CRYSTAL, by M. S. Chaning-Pearce (1940)
—contains a section on J. C. Powys, pp. 180-193.

THE LIFE OF LLEWELYN POWYS, by M. Elvin (1946)
—new edition, 1953.

THE NEW SPIRIT, ed. E. W. Martin (1946)
—contains a chapter on Llewelyn Powys, pp. 42-53.

'The Path of T. F. Powys', by R. C. Churchill in *The Critic* (Spring,
1947).

LIVING WRITERS, edited by G. H. Phelps (1947)
—a broadcast symposium which contains an essay on T. F. Powys,
pp. 151-157.

THE BROTHERS POWYS, by L. Wilkinson. Cincinnati (1947)
—reprinted in *Essays by Divers Hands*, 1948.
'J. C. Powys', by K. Hopkins in *World Review* (March, 1958).
'Llewelyn Powys: A village Radical' by W. G. Allen in *The Wind and the Rain* (Winter, 1949).

SEVEN FRIENDS, by L. Marlow (1953).

CATALOGUE OF MANUSCRIPTS OF LLEWELYN POWYS, by G. F. Simms. Hurst, Berks. (1953).
'The Quiet Man of Dorset' [T. F. Powys] by F. Powys in *The Adelphi* (Fourth Quarter, 1954).
J. C. Powys Number of *Dock Leaves*, ed. by R. Garlick. (Spring, 1956).
'A Famous Family', by A. Gregory in *The London Magazine* (March 1958).

T. F. POWYS, by H. Coombes (1960).

THE MODERN AGE, edited by B. Ford (1961)
—in Pelican Books: contains a chapter on T. F. Powys and Dylan Thomas, pp. 415-428.
'Lawrence, Joyce and [J.C.] Powys,' by G. Wilson Knight, in *Essays in Criticism* (October 1961).

WRITERS AND THEIR WORK

General Editor: BONAMY DOBRÉE

The first 55 issues in the Series appeared under the General Editorship of T. O. BEACHCROFT

Sixteenth Century and Earlier:
FRANCIS BACON: J. Max Patrick
CHAUCER: Nevill Coghill
ENGLISH MARITIME WRITING:
   Hakluyt to Cook: Oliver Warner
MALORY: M. C. Bradbrook
MARLOWE: Philip Henderson
SIDNEY: Kenneth Muir
SKELTON: Peter Green
SPENSER: Rosemary Freeman
WYATT: Sergio Baldi

Seventeenth Century:
SIR THOMAS BROWNE: Peter Green
BUNYAN: Henri Talon
CAVALIER POETS: Robin Skelton
DONNE: Frank Kermode
DRYDEN: Bonamy Dobrée
HERRICK: John Press
HOBBES: T. E. Jessop
BEN JONSON: J. B. Bamborough
LOCKE: Maurice Cranston
ANDREW MARVELL: John Press
MILTON: E. M. W. Tillyard
SHAKESPEARE: C. J. Sisson
SHAKESPEARE:
  CHRONICLES: Clifford Leach
  EARLY COMEDIES: Derek Traversi
  GREAT TRAGEDIES: Kenneth Muir
  LATE COMEDIES: G. K. Hunter
  PROBLEM PLAYS: Peter Ure
THREE METAPHYSICAL POETS:
             Margaret Willy
IZAAK WALTON: Margaret Bottrall

Eighteenth Century:
BERKELEY: T. E. Jessop
BLAKE: Kathleen Raine
BOSWELL: P. A. W. Collins
BURKE: T. E. Utley
BURNS: David Daiches
COWPER: N. Nicholson
CRABBE: R. L. Brett
DEFOE: J. R. Sutherland

ENGLISH HYMNS: Arthur Pollard
FIELDING: John Butt
GIBBON: C. V. Wedgwood
GOLDSMITH: A. Norman Jeffares
GRAY: R. W. Ketton-Cremer
JOHNSON: S. C. Roberts
POPE: Ian Jack
RICHARDSON: R. F. Brissenden
SHERIDAN: W. A. Darlington
CHRISTOPHER SMART:
            Geoffrey Grigson
SMOLLETT: Laurence Brander
STEELE, ADDISON AND THEIR
 PERIODICAL ESSAYS:
         A. R. Humphreys
STERNE: D. W. Jefferson
SWIFT: J. Middleton Murry
HORACE WALPOLE: Hugh Honour

Nineteenth Century:
MATTHEW ARNOLD: Kenneth Allott
JANE AUSTEN: S. Townsend Warner
THE BRONTE SISTERS:
            Phyllis Bentley
BROWNING: John Bryson
SAMUEL BUTLER: G. D. H. Cole
BYRON: Herbert Read
CARLYLE: David Gascoyne
LEWIS CARROLL: Derek Hudson
COLERIDGE: Kathleen Raine
DICKENS: K. J. Fielding
DISRAELI: Paul Bloomfield
GEORGE ELIOT: Lettice Cooper
ENGLISH TRAVELLERS IN THE NEAR
  EAST: Robin Fedden
FITZGERALD: Joanna Richardson
MRS. GASKELL: Miriam Allott
GISSING: A. C. Ward
THOMAS HARDY: R. A. Scott-James
HAZLITT: J. B. Priestley
G. M. HOPKINS: Geoffrey Grigson
T. H. HUXLEY: William Irvine
KEATS: Edmund Blunden
LAMB: Edmund Blunden

LANDOR: G. Rostrevor Hamilton
MACAULAY: G. R. Potter
JOHN STUART MILL: M. Cranston
WILLIAM MORRIS: P. Henderson
NEWMAN: J. M. Cameron
PATER: Iain Fletcher
ROSSETTI: Oswald Doughty
RUSKIN: Peter Quennell
SIR WALTER SCOTT: Ian Jack
SHELLEY: Stephen Spender
R. L. STEVENSON: G. B. Stern
SWINBURNE: H. J. C. Grierson
TENNYSON: F. L. Lucas
THACKERAY: Laurence Brander
FRANCIS THOMPSON: P. Butter
TROLLOPE: Hugh Sykes Davies
OSCAR WILDE: James Laver
WORDSWORTH: Helen Darbishire

Twentieth Century:

W. H. AUDEN: Richard Hoggart
HILAIRE BELLOC: Renée Haynes
ARNOLD BENNETT: F. Swinnerton
EDMUND BLUNDEN: Alec M. Hardie
ELIZABETH BOWEN: Jocelyn Brooke
ROBERT BRIDGES: J. Sparrow
ROY CAMPBELL: David Wright
JOYCE CARY: Walter Allen
G. K. CHESTERTON: C. Hollis
WINSTON CHURCHILL: John Connell
R.G. COLLINGWOOD: E.W.F. Tomlin
I. COMPTON-BURNETT:
          Pamela Hansford Johnson
JOSEPH CONRAD: Oliver Warner
WALTER DE LA MARE: K. Hopkins
THE DETECTIVE STORY IN
          BRITAIN: Julian Symons
NORMAN DOUGLAS: Ian Greenlees
T. S. ELIOT: M. C. Bradbrook
FORD MADOX FORD: Kenneth Young
E. M. FORSTER: Rex Warner

CHRISTOPHER FRY: Derek Stanford
JOHN GALSWORTHY: R. H. Mottram
ROBERT GRAVES: M. Seymour Smith
GRAHAM GREENE: Francis Wyndham
L. P. HARTLEY AND ANTHONY POW-
     ELL: P. Bloomfield and B. Bergonzi
A. E. HOUSMAN: Ian Scott-Kilvert
ALDOUS HUXLEY: Jocelyn Brooke
HENRY JAMES: Michael Swan
JAMES JOYCE: J. I. M. Stewart
RUDYARD KIPLING: B. Dobrée
D. H. LAWRENCE: Kenneth Young
C. DAY LEWIS: Clifford Dyment
WYNDHAM LEWIS: E. W. F. Tomlin
KATHERINE MANSFIELD: Ian Gordon
JOHN MASEFIELD: L. A. G. Strong
SOMERSET MAUGHAM: J. Brophy
EDWIN MUIR: J. C. Hall
J. MIDDLETON MURRY: Philip Mairet
GEORGE ORWELL: Tom Hopkinson
POETS OF THE 1939-45 WAR:
                    R. N. Currey
J. B. PRIESTLEY: Ivor Brown
HERBERT READ: Francis Berry
BERTRAND RUSSELL: Alan Dorward
BERNARD SHAW: A. C. Ward
EDITH SITWELL: John Lehmann
OSBERT SITWELL: Roger Fulford
C. P. SNOW: William Cooper
LYTTON STRACHEY:
               R. A. Scott-James
DYLAN THOMAS: G. S. Fraser
G. M. TREVELYAN: J. H. Plumb
WAR POETS: 1914-18:
               Edmund Blunden
EVELYN WAUGH: Christopher Hollis
H. G. WELLS: Montgomery Belgion
CHARLES WILLIAMS:
               John Heath-Stubbs
VIRGINIA WOOLF: Bernard Blackstone
W. B. YEATS: G. S. Fraser

In Preparation:

MEREDITH: Phyllis Bartlett
J. M. SYNGE and LADY GREGORY:
               Elizabeth Coxhead

SHAKESPEARE: THE HISTORIES:
               L. C. Knights
RONALD FIRBANK and JOHN
   BETJEMAN: Jocelyn Brooke